UNIVERSAL LAW
for the Aquarian Age

DR. FRANK ALPER

ARIZONA METAPHYSICAL SOCIETY
P.O. BOX 44027, PHOENIX, AZ 85064

Copyright © 1986 by Dr. Frank Alper

Arizona Metaphysical Society
P.O. Box 44027
Phoenix, AZ 85064

No part of this book may be reproduced by any mechanical, photographic, or electronic process, or in the form of a phonographic recording, nor may it be stored in a retrieval system, transmitted, or otherwise be copied for public or private use — other than for "fair use" without written permission of the publisher.

ISBN 1-55705-074-0

Contents

Introduction vi
Law 1
Universal Law. 7
Stealing 17
Greed. 21
Sin 27
Guilt. 33
Vanity 35
Private Domain. 39
Exchange 41
Self-Denial. 45
Coveting 49
Spiritual Union 51
Personal Morality. 55
Responsibility to Ego. 59
Fertility and Reproduction 63

Responsibility to Offspring	65
Celibacy	69
Isolation	73
Incarnation	77
Personality	81
Hate	87
Acquisition	91
Negativity	95
Spiritual Law	105
Reality	106
Cause and Effect	107
Acceptance	109
Karma	110
Judgment	110
Soul Evolution	112
Fidelity	113
Christ Light	115
Ten Commandments	117

Prelude

I am the Lord thy God. I speak to My Children on the planet Earth in Love Eternal. Within the written words here inscribed, are My Truth and messages to Mankind.

You are all preparing for the coming years ahead. My Beloved Son is within all of My Children. Allow His Presence to make your lives enriched beyond your dreams.

Heed Me, My Children. Open your hearts to eternal life. I am with you, each and every one for eternity.

May the Divine Presence of Creation shine on the core of your souls and Light your way to the final assimilation.

I am Michael Sananda, The Spirit of the Universal Christ.

I am the Lord thy God.

Introduction

Many aspects of universal law have been channeled to me during the past several years. This book is a compilation of those spiritual energies in their original context.

Universal law is an expanding and contracting vibration, always in motion. This tells us that each individual is responsible for his own interpretation of the law and its application in his life. If, after an action is taken, an error has been made, it can be corrected by another action called karma. This constitutes the growth of mankind.

These laws have been assimilated to stimulate your minds and assist you in determining your truth. If this can be accomplished, then we have served you well.

Law

Law is a vibration set into place as a regulatory agent to assist mankind in their growth and in the course of their lives. Law is established not so much as a restrictive measure as it is a guideline, to assist one in the selection of a proper path and to help one avoid error in the pursuit of one's life. Law is not established to punish or to take away.

Many relate to Law as a "limiting" vibration, something that tends to confine them and hold them down. Perhaps if mankind looked at it from another perspective, looked at the Law as the first step up the ladder, as information given to mankind to help them begin a path with direction, then the Law would become a useful tool for mankind, rather than something to rebel against and avoid.

Law changes. As the awareness of mankind rises, the need for change in Law also arises. I cannot establish a general rule and say, "As mankind grows Law becomes less restrictive," for this is not always so. I can say that as Law changes, the room for free expression increases, leaving more to the responsibility of the individual to make proper decisions. And, as all know, with awareness and knowledge comes responsibility.

Law, as it was set into vibrational existence millennia ago, has changed, grown, and developed. As the soul grows and develops, the Law must expand to accommodate this growth. You receive, at a stage in your development, a partial Law. As you grow, more and more of the scope of the total Law is revealed to you to facilitate your understanding and comprehension of the Law. For these reasons, many of the ancient interpretations do not apply, verbatim, at this time of existence.

At times, a child accepts a physical incarnation to serve a special role for his Father. When the child has reached maturity within the incarnation and is ready to assume the Service Contract, a covenant is established between him and his Father at the conscious level.

When you are asked to place your entire being and welfare in the hands of your Father, when you are asked to walk His path and allow Him to guide and steer you, a release is effected. No longer are you totally responsible only to yourself, for within the covenant you and your Father are One. Your responsibilities are now joint responsibilities. This applies to every action you undertake during the course of the balance of your life.

Man refers to this as a relinquishing of his "free will." Is it truly a relinquishing, or is it a blending of purpose and will with that of your Father, to acknowledge the oneness?

The key to the apprehension involved in

making this covenant is self-worth; it is the faith in your ability to be worthy of the Oneness. Once this has been conquered, the actual mechanics of establishing and accepting the covenant become simple, for it is the act of your progression.

Universal Law

My Laws pertaining to the Universe do not have the same meaning or context as the Ten Commandments or Laws of Moses that relate to humanity on Earth.

Every planet in this Universe that contains life—both life as you know it and life as it is unfamiliar to you—has a series of "Commandments" pertaining to the civilizations on that specific planet. It should be fairly evident that these Laws are not designed to apply universally, for variations in Law are necessary according to the existing energy patterns assigned to each planet.

It is for this reason that as time elapses, as humanity's vibrations begin to rise, the interpretation of the Law applying to civilizations on Earth change and expand to adapt to the growth and codes of societies. This enables the Law to be compatible with, not contradictory to, the codes of incarnated life.

Universal Law does not vary. It has great flexibility in its scope, but it does not vary. Universal Law relates to the growth and vibrations of the soul, and necessitates the stability of the Law to ensure the uniformity of the pattern of growth of all souls.

The most important Universal Law is that all, and I streess all, is always in "Divine

Order." What does this mean to you? It means that there are no "accidents" relating to your true, spiritual existence. It means that everything takes place in your life exactly at the time it is to occur, and in the capacity and degree to which it is meant to occur. If this were not so, the vibrations within any given situation on any planet, solar system, or galaxy would be thrown out of balance. This cannot be allowed to take place.

    If, within the Divine Plan for the evolution of a planet, a large group of people were at one level of spiritual evolution when they should be at another level, the vibrations of that planet would not be in Order. This would result in imbalance of the plan of growth and evolution on that planet.

There are times when unusual situations do occur. For example, there are many souls incarnated on your planet and other planets who make great strides in their growth at the conscious level. When this occurs, their destiny for service in that incarnation is often altered to allow for further service during that lifetime.

There are many who undergo "transfusions" of energy by being exposed to the "Universal Christ Light" to a much greater degree than the average human being. This enables them to carry an expansive quality of the Light to assist them in their work. These alterations do not affect the Divine Plan as they are in the classification of what are called "Additives." They do not alter the vibrational flow, but rather enhance it while maintaining the same direction and flow. This preserves the consistency of the Divine Plan.

The Law is the Law. Every single vibration of Universal Law was established at exactly the same moment. From the instant of its establishment, it has never altered by even one vibration in its basic structure. This has ensured the continuity and flow of the Law. The Law has expanded in stature and scope but not in basic principle.

Let me state several Laws that originate at the Universal level: "If a soul has incurred and completed an incarnation without achieving a new level of growth, by not adding to its vibrations during the course of the incarnation, it must assume another incarnation almost immediately."

I shall explain. This condition relates directly to the Law of Progression. All is always in a constant state of movement. If a soul is not constantly expanding its vibrations by exposing itself to new energies, its energies shall begin to dissipate. A soul may not remain stationary, for nothing is at rest. All is in a state of movement in a forward or a dissipating vibrationary spiral.

For this reason, a soul who has not added growth to its vibrations during the course of an incarnation must incarnate almost immediately for the preservation of its prior evolution. If not, it shall become involved in a slow regression of its frequencies.

When I say to you, "it must," I do not

wish to infer that the Father, or one of the soul's "advisers," orders this action. It is the self, the awareness of the soul, that instigates this action. It is of the soul's own free will, as it realizes and is aware of the consequences of failing to correct its errors.

Another Universal Law is: "No soul is permitted to transverse levels of vibrations within the realms of heaven, but must remain within a level compatible with its own vibration." This may appear to be a restrictive Law. It may seem as if there is a hierarchy or caste system, but this is not the purpose for the Law. If a soul of a lower level of vibration were to enter an incompatible sphere of vibrations, it could affect the Universal flow and result in what mankind calls a "short circuit" and be destroyed. For this reason, this Law must be rigidly maintained.

The result is the establishment of definite levels of vibrations. Perhaps you have experienced situations where you have requested information from one of your spiritual advisers and a delay in the answer has occurred. He or she might have had to seek, through progressive channels, the answer from one who is in a higher frequency.

If an individual comes to you and asks you to make contact with a loved one who has passed, you are not in Order if you "scan the heavens" to locate this soul. You must seek spiritual counsel, and request that the proper frequency level assist you in locating this soul and have it brought to your level of vibration to establish the communication.

The most rigid and inflexible Universal Law is one that you are familiar with. It is also one of the Laws related to Moses and applies throughout the Universe. The Law states: "Thou shalt love thy Father, the Lord thy God, with all thy heart, with all thy soul, and with all thy might, and there shall be no other gods before Me."

The violation of this Law is the single greatest cause of karma that the soul encounters. I wish you to understand that this Law was not established for your Father to sit and accept homage and adoration from His children. It was established so that all of His children would come to the understanding of His energies within them. To assist them in accepting, at all levels, that they and their Father are One. That they are an expression of the Lord, and that they need no other. All they need is the understanding and recognition of the blending of their energies into Oneness. Denial of this is the most repetitious expression of karma for mankind.

Stealing

During the time of Moses, this Law was interpreted to mean, "Thou shalt not take what visibly and physically is not yours." This aspect of this Law is still in force. However, the scope of the Law has increased a hundred-fold. Today we are aware of those who would take of your vibrations, who would attempt to transmute your love into negativity, drain you of strength, tempt you, and try to sway you from your path. A vibration is sacred unto one who has nourished it. One who "steals" vibrations draws a most severe experience unto himself.

Perhaps the Law in today's context should be reworded thus: "Thou shalt obey the Laws of Substance and Prosperity." If all practiced the Laws of Substance and Prosperity, the word **steal** would not apply in any language. All would understand that Substance is in a constant state of flow, that all one's needs are available to be drawn from the Universal Substance as the need is created and expressed. The need to steal arises when one tries to retain Substance, to hold on to it, to stop the flow, to amass the Substance by considering it his or hers. This creates greed, the desire to hoard, and leads to the urge to steal. If man will accept that he is merely a channel for Substance to flow to, and then through, he will find peace, for his needs shall be fulfilled.

To steal is to interrupt the flow of Universal Substance. For this, one most assuredly draws karma. Know that the karma is not for the act of stealing, but for the act of interrupting the flow of Substance.

Greed

We talk of the Laws of Prosperity, Substance, and Flow. We are all aware that in order for the Law of Prosperity to function properly, it is necessary to continue the flow unbroken. You are not to erect a dam in the stream to stem the flow of water, but to keep the stream free from debris so that the flow may continue uninterrupted. Periodically, one comes along who builds a dam, and the name of the dam is "greed."

Greed is not confined to involvements with money. It is involved with property and estate, with animals and other possessions. It is involved within personalities, for people conceive in their minds that they possess people. So, we find that the greatest offense that we label **greed** is involved in the interrelationship of people. It occurs when we do not allow freedom of expression for those whom we love and share our lives with. We wish to hold on to them in our preconceived concepts and thought patterns, for our own insecurities prevent us from allowing them their own expression. We do this out of fear, least we lose them. In doing so, we stop the flow and cause agitation, resentments, and blockages. Our lives become stifled and our growth is considerably hampered.

The man who walks with his Father, who unites his energies with his Father's Love, need never suffer frustrations and anxieties and has no cause to become involved in the energies of greed. So, the substance flows smoothly, to and from, and to, again.

This Universal Law never varies. It is a constant. How many do you know who have hoarded out of greed, who have retained what they have hoarded, and lost it all, in time? In essence, they have denied their oneness with their Father; for they have not trusted in His flow of Substance.

Throughout your reading of the Bible, there are examples time and time again pointing to lack of faith in flow. It resulted in severe hardships. What would have happened if Pharaoh had released the Hebrews at Moses's first request, if he had faith that God's Will be done, instead of holding on to the supply at hand, the supply of labor and slaves? Egypt would have continued to flourish instead of undergoing devastation and ruin for many, many years.

This example has been repeated time and time again. Look at your world as it exists for you now, with nation upon nation striving to amass munitions and to hold on to positions of power, instead of releasing and allowing flow.

The greatest greed involves greed toward self. This is demonstrated in the unwillingness of man to release himself to his Father's care, and in his insistence on holding on to what he thinks he possesses in the way of material things and emotional attachments.

So I say to you, my children, you who strive to become enlightened, to become one with self, have faith, release yourself to your Father. You shall not fail. You shall rise, and your flow of Substance shall continue to grow and increase.

Sin

The Book of Leviticus contains a category of paragraphs describing lists of many sins that man commits, or has committed, and the penance or punishment assigned to each particular sin. For centuries mankind has lived in fear, not so much in fear of what he considered God, but more in fear of what he considered sin, without even bothering to find out what the word meant and where it had its origin.

Historians refer to the original sin in the symbolism of Eve biting the apple, the forbidden fruit. Was this a sin, or was it symbolically freedom of choice?

Is it a sin to steal, or is it a free-will decision that draws to the individual a severe experience, the lesson being of a nature of the individual's own choosing?

Man says that the master Jesus died on the cross for all the sins of mankind. Did this relieve man of his obligations to his Father? Did this free man from his lessons of growth and experience? Most assuredly not. What sins did Jesus die for? If man truly needs to have a sin, then let there be only one, and let that one be a lack of belief in God. For if, indeed, I AM is your only reality and all else is a projection in constant change, then that can be the only sin.

The Bible talks of the vengeance of the Lord. Through periods of history, it has been said that He has "smitten" those who have sinned, that He has hurled tempests, floods, and bolts of lightning to punish man. There is a passage that states, "vengeance is Mine, sayeth the Lord." His energies are energies of Divine Love. Those who err in their ways draw to them their own justice, bring to themselves their own degree of lesson. They know at the soul level the degree of vibration they have misused, and the degree of balancing vibration that is necessary to restore the equilibrium. This is Universal Law. Vengeance does not exist, for if it did exist, the energies of your Father would not be a constant, but a variable, and your world would be in total chaos.

Why then did the sages, the ancient rabbis, put so much stress on the word sin? The people were weak; their minds and their truth vascillated from day to day. There was a need for a weapon, a weapon to bind the people together. They chose to accomplish this with fear. The fear they chose to hold the people together was the word sin.

Why did your Father allow this to occur? Why did He not stop this at its inception? It was the choice of the leaders to take this action. The Father did not wish to interfere. The free will of man must be given exercise and freedom. If not, he shall not grow. You know that any action that is taken in your truth is not sinful, draws to you no lesson, and is only an experience for you. If you are unaware of the proper course of action due to lack of exposure to a situation, then you are accountable to yourself to learn, to learn from the experience, so that it shall not occur again.

The Laws relating to sin in the Book of Leviticus do not pertain to mankind at the present time. If it were possible to erase the word **sin** whenever it is written and replace it with the word **lesson**, I would ask that it be done. Man has evolved to the point where he no longer needs to relate to His Father's energies in fear. He can relate openly in Love and accept his errors.

The solution to the problem of sin is quite simple. If you will take the step forward and accept the Father's presence within you, and accept His guidance in all facets of your life, you need never be concerned, for you shall know that you are walking in Truth and Love. All your actions and decisions shall be taken in "Your" vibrations, for at that moment you and He shall be as One, and your purpose and actions shall be as One. You need never again concern yourselves with the energies that are called sin.

Guilt

Is the word **guilt** synonomous with the word sin? In many ways it is. What causes guilt? Inadequacy, a lack of strength within your faith and your convictions? Perhaps it is making your decisions too quickly, resulting in second thoughts that allow you to feel guilty for a choice you have made. Once having decided that you are guilty, you might as well say that you have "sinned."

You have no right to "guilt." You have no right to regret an action. You must take your actions only when they are your truth, and if you cannot determine which course of action is your truth, postpone the action until you can.

The time has arrived for mankind to release the energies of self-punishment and lack of self-worth. He must stand strong and firm. He must move forward in a positive direction and recognize that he is an instrument of Love, and Love alone.

An action taken in good faith needs no remorse. A negative result from an action taken in good faith must not lead to regrets, only to an awareness of the outcome, and a new pattern of decisions for future actions.

Vanity

If we take ourselves back to biblical days, we find that the ancients left their hair unshorn. Who was man to cast away what God had bestowed upon him? Indeed, for that time, that was their truth. If a man would have had his locks shorn he would have been ostracized, perhaps even stoned. How does this apply today? It does not. There are many areas of orthodoxy in religions throughout the world where the hair is not shorn, where artificial means applied to the body for beauty are forbidden, for this is their truth. But the evolvement of mankind, both intellectually and spiritually, has brought us to the point where man realizes that these small things do not place one in a position of turning from God, nor do they prove one's devotion to God. So, it has become a matter of free will and taste, basically relating to where one is in the position of one's life. Generally speaking, those who are involved deeply within the material, social vibrations are more prone to utilize this cosmetic method of beauty and prolonging of superficial youth. The importance of these things wanes as one moves into elevated spiritual vibrations. Then, one understands that the true beauty shows from within.

In some areas of life we may come to a

point of conflict with vanity. Is it vanity, or is it care of self? Is it vain for one to exercise to keep one's physical body trim and firm? The vanity comes into play when we determine the purpose for the course of action. If the accent is overly stressed in the vibrations of vanity whereby one's growth and balance of life suffer, then indeed the individual is in error.

As you grow, you shall find that the aging process becomes of total unimportance to you, that your relationship with this process fades away and you just are, and can just be. At this point, the energies of vanity assume a minor role in your emotional expression.

To surgically alter one's physical temple reinforces the illusion of self-accceptance and oneness with the Father's Essence. He asks no sacrifice of mankind to enter the realms of perfection. All He seeks is you, unadorned, in your Truth.

Private Domain

Each man is entitled to own and amass property, whether it be a single plot of land, a large area, a state, a country, an island, as long as he has procured it by honorable methods and hard work. No one is required to be denied assets. No one is required to be destitute, or suffer from any lack, in order to prove one's devotion to the Father. All are entitled to acquire possessions. All are allowed and encouraged to protect their possessions and their property in honor, and by honorable means.

If within the Law of Private Domain one abuses the flow of substance that has come to him, one shall surely lose it. All must understand and know that all substance is in a constant state of flow and never rests. It is acquired to be used fruitfully and productively. If, once acquired, it is allowed to lie fallow, it soon dissipates.

The most prosperous child is the one who walks with the Lord. What else could man possess that by sacrificing would bring him closer to God?

Exchange

The Law states: "If an individual utilizes and exercises the energies of sharing with another human being, then he must make himself available and open to receive like energies in return."

A simple Law, and yet one of the most difficult for mankind to observe properly. Man is brought up from childhood to learn to "give and take." That is the key, the words *give and take*, a bad choice of combination of letters, for there is only sharing. The word *give* involves a form of sacrifice. The word take implies drawing to one's self without permission.

If one wishes to return energies to you, to share with you, you are not taking, you are receiving. You are allowing others to exercise the same vibrations that you yourself have exercised, and you have no right to deny them this.

The Law of Exchange also embodies the following words: "It is every individual's responsibility to own himself or herself totally. When one attempts to "give of himself" to another, he opens himself to vulnerability and may create karma.

The action of mankind is to share. In this manner, the recipient is able to receive a greater portion of your energies without any loss of your strength, stability, and self-ownership.

The Law of Exchange falls under the vibrations of the Law of Prosperity. If one shares and denies a return of the flow, he has stopped the flow of his prosperity. Your teachers share with you of their energies and their knowledge. The young student who does not have the ability to exchange energies at equal levels may find another method of exchange: a blessing, a basket of fruit, an exchange of currency, or a passing of information to others. They exchange upon receiving so that others may exchange and allow more and more to receive.

Create a world of growth where no one takes, only shares in the flow of Life and Love.

If you are to assume your role within the spiritual vibrations, you must observe the Law of Exchange; until you do, you are restricting your vibrations.

Self-Denial

The Law states: "He who judges himself unworthy shall indeed be denied worthiness. He who deems himself worthy shall flow in the mainstream of prosperity." Man is a multi-level being. The conscious mind, with its insecurities, may decide that it is unworthy of energies that are coming to it. But what is unworthiness? Is it fear? Is it lack of self-confidence? Is it awe? It is all of them! In essence, it is judgment—judgment of self.

We have spoken to you before of the areas of suffering. You have heard many times that your Father is Divine Love and is incapable of imposing suffering upon you. Therefore, the imposition of suffering is truly your own manifestation. Denial is the imposition of suffering. To say to yourself that you are unworthy, and therefore you must suffer and do without, is self-denial. Whom are you unworthy in relation to? There is no one to compare yourself to but you. You are your Temple. You have no right to deny the flow, the fluidity to the God within you.

Some will say that they deny themselves out of humility. They wish to be humble. They do not wish to give the impression that they are greedy or walking in ego, so they deny themselves. They are judging others' reactions to them. For this decision, they are indeed walking in ego, for they are placing themselves in a position of ascertaining that they know the reactions of others before they occur. Deny yourselves nothing. Receive all that is offered and tendered to you, for it is all yours. Allow it to come to you with open arms, experience it, utilize it, and allow others to receive it from you.

Coveting

In ancient days this Law was interpreted to an extreme literal degree. One would not approach a friend's wife. If a chance meeting occurred, both would go their separate ways. Communication and association were frowned upon except in the presence of the spouses.

Today we understand far more. Today mankind is aware of the sensing of vibrations, of the sensing of a different aspect of their lives. Man is encouraged to "love thy neighbor's wife." I speak of love, within this area, in terms of spiritual vibrations, of walking with one's heart open so that others may feel and share your love, to unashamedly extend and offer it to all; not to walk with your arms crossing your chest, hiding yourself from your fellow man, containing what you have to offer inside of yourself instead of sharing freely with your brothers and sisters.

The word **covet** means desire, desire in a carnal sense. You are awakened Children of Light, aware of your identities. You no longer have the capacity to be carnal within your emotions, for if you attempted to do so, it would destroy you.

You are expressions of your vibrations. You are expressions of your love. Not one of you should carry shame for this.

Spiritual Union

The Law states: "When a relationship between two souls has been established by the blending and union of spiritual vibrations, the relationship shall be blessed by our Father and shall perpetuate itself."

What does this mean to the average man? What it means is this: When two are involved in a relationship and have as a foundation and basic principle of this relationship a spiritual union of vibrations, this relationship shall be blessed by their Father and shall endure, never dissipate, and always remain constant and fulfilling. When two people enter into a relationship based on conscious emotional involvement, whether it be sexual or expressed in other physical areas, it shall be entered into because of the lessons involved between the two souls. If within this relationship a spiritual relationship does not occur, the relationship shall dissipate and eventually end.

This is why I say to you that marriage is a union of vibrations, not of emotions. Why is it that so many men and women who are married seek elsewhere for fulfillment for themselves? They do this because they have placed themselves in a limiting situation that does not allow them the fulfillment that they need at all levels of their existence. They have entered the relationship without a solid foundation and reasoning.

I do not mean to imply that there is only one person with whom you can establish a spiritual union, for this is not true. There are many with whom a spiritual compatibility is possible. The key is the awareness and the sensitivity to recognize this compatibility when it appears to you; then you shall have a relationship without frustrations, jealousies, and anger. It will be one of trust and harmony and love, for the knowledge will be there that the vibrations shall not change, but shall be constant.

Personal Morality

The Law states: "An individual must set standards for his moral behavior in accordance with his own truth. If, however, his truth is diametrically opposed to the laws set down by the society in which he lives, he must either adjust his moral behavior or relocate himself to a society that is compatible with his beliefs."

No man has the right to set moral standards for another, for no man walks in another man's truth. When you have established a moral code for yourself and you violate it, you draw a lesson to yourself. You have, of course, imposed it upon yourself, for you have set your truth and violated it and must take the responsibility for your actions.

What are you supposed to do if, within your truth, you desire to take an action that others do not believe is proper? The answer is quite clearly defined. If in taking this action others will consciously suffer and you are aware of this, you shall draw a lesson to yourself if you take the action. If you take the action in such a manner that others do not suffer as a result of the action, then it is proper for you to do so, for it is your truth. The line becomes quite fine at times, and yet it is there. No one is intended ever to be denied the expression of his truth, but the circumstance and conditions must be proper for its expression.

Responsibility to Ego

This may sound like a strange Law, but it is a reality, for ego is a reality. Perhaps I should begin by giving you the definition of ego.

"Ego is an emotional reaction or response based on a previous experience within a given situation or circumstance." What is man's responsibility to his ego?

Is man to totally suppress his ego? By no means, for by doing so he puts a chain around the expression of his conscious personality. He eliminates the factor necessary to motivate him and assist him to achieve his goals. The expression of ego is valid, for it exists. The key is, at what point on the scale of its expression is he within a safety factor? The answer is, when man will utilize ego as a tool for growth and expression, it is proper. When the ego utilizes man to achieve its end, he is involved in an improper situation.

Many times I am saddened to see one who has grown spiritually and has achieved a certain amount of success and fame, then has allowed his ego to break free and take control and move the life out of perspective. Many times this will cause a Child to be lost to his Father. It is for this reason that many times doubts are placed in your mind, doubts as to the validity of your truth, your spiritual communication, to force you to keep your ego in perspective, to remind you that you are not perfect. Do not try to hide your pleasures and emotions; express them and enjoy them, for many times they are a return of energy for much effort and energy expended. However, know that the time for elation and back-slapping has a limit, and when its expression is over, your work must continue.

Fertility and Reproduction

The Law states: "Neither man nor woman has the right to alter himself or herself in any manner or form that will prevent the conception and birth of a child. Let it be known that if it is your Father's desire that a child be born, the child shall be born. If it is not within the pattern of incarnation for the parents, the child shall not be born."

This Law has created much controversy over the ages. I do not sit here and say to you that it is your obligation to follow this Law to the letter, for, as with most Laws, one must adapt it to one's own truth. The important thing is to understand the basic principle behind the Law. This principle is: "At all times, God's Will will be done." One might say, "In my truth, I firmly believe I am not to have any more children and therefore it is my truth to alter myself to prevent this from coming to pass." Who is to say you are wrong? But then again, who is to say that you would have conceived any more children in the first place? How many women have conceived and given birth to children where doctors have said birth is impossible?

Do what you believe you must do, but do it in your truth. Always bear in mind that God's Will be done.

Responsibility to Offspring

Where does parents' responsibility to their offspring begin, and where does it end? If it is true that mankind's prime responsibility is to the self, then how can they justify so much self-sacrifice for their children? This is present not only during their formative years, but many carry it with them for the balance of their lives. In biblical days, when a boy reached the age of thirteen years, he was considered a man and was free to be responsible for himself and for his actions, always to be respectful to his parents but to pursue his life and be responsible for it.

Today, children at the age of thirteen are far more mature and wise than were their counterparts in ancient days. Yet, in many cases they are tightly controlled and held down by parental authority. The key to the proper attitude is to understand that your child is a person, an individual who is with you for a while, and who upon maturity assumes responsibility for his own life and actions. At that moment, the essence of the parents' responsibility has ended, and they begin to serve in the capacity of a friend and adviser.

Many parents hold on too tightly during the formative years and it becomes too difficult to release at the proper time, so both the parent and the child suffer. It becomes increasingly more important with each generation for the parent to understand his role in relation to the child, for the children are coming in more and more aware and need freedom of expression to enable them to remain open spiritually.

Celibacy

The Law states: "When a Child of Light consciously accepts his identity and pledges his life and his service to his Father, in the pledging of this service he automatically assumes a vow of celibacy, at a spiritual level."

By this I mean: "I shall love my Father with all my heart, with all my soul, and with all my might, and there shall be no other Gods before me. I shall not desecrate this vow or pledge by endearing myself to any other form, shape, or manner of God, or idol or article to worship. I shall be true in all aspects of my spiritual growth to my Divine Father."

One may ask, if this is the case, why is it that so many men of the cloth are required to assume an oath of physical celibacy? Let us return to ancient days, to the days of sacrifice, when the level of development required a different form of commitment to our Father: the sacrifice of a lamb, the offering of gold and precious gems, and the forsaking of physical pleasures. One had to be willing to sacrifice to prove devotion and dedication to our Father. But, as I have stated before, times change, and interpretations of laws expand and grow with the vibrations.

As I stand here this day, I say to you that if, at your level of development, it is necessary for you to assume physical celibacy to prove your devotion to your Father, you are not too worthy in the first place.

Celibacy in the physical sense is caused by fear. One might say that if one is not tempted, then one will not stray from one's path. So we find that a lack of belief in self causes one to deprive oneself of a normal function of life, an expression of love. If one can understand and practice the Law of Spiritual Celibacy, one shall never have a problem with expressing himself physically. The understanding will be there, and the temptations shall dissipate and never cause problems.

You may apply celibacy to diet, to abstaining from meat, spirits, or tobacco.

What does abstinence in these areas prove? It proves that you have a need to overcome what you unconsciously feel is a shortcoming, so you create a situation to prove devotion and dedication: a situation without substance and without foundation. Can one man say to another that he is unworthy because he eats meat?

Remember, my children, your spiritual master may be the alcoholic lying in the gutter in the throes of a lesson. Keep your vows of celibacy where they belong, in relation to your spiritual commitment to your Father.

Isolation

The Law states: "When an individual embarks on a path of spiritual growth and allows the flow of knowledge and vibrations to come to him, he must allow the vibrations to continue and flow on through him. If he stops the flow to contain them within himself and for himself, the flow shall cease."

In essence, what I am saying to you is that if you spend years studying and growing and decide that you have become such a spiritual being that you cannot and do not wish to relate to others, but wish to sit in seclusion to meditate, study, and bask in your knowledge and glory, you shall soon have nothing to bask in. The vibrations of knowledge that flow to you are not yours. They are part of the flow of Universal Substance. You may take your boat and ride in the waves of energy, to assimilate it. But it is not within your power to divert the stream, to stop the flow. You are as a waystation, a transfer point, nothing more.

When one utilizes another's energies to gain knowledge for himself, and refuses to pass on this knowledge and energy to others, a regression takes place within his vibration. Before too long, he has returned to the beginning. It is not for my children to sit and grow in isolation. Your service is within the masses of humanity, not in isolated meditation or amid the peace of your peers. I do not ask you to combine your energies with them, only to relate to them and nurture them.

In the pure abstraction, you are all nothing but a thought, an idea, a projection. Therefore, you are in a constant fluid state. It is not within your rights to take the fluid flow and create a solid.

Incarnation

The Law states: "When a soul is created, its book of records is established and a total pattern of learning and growth is established for the soul."

This pattern is not firmly fixed, but is quite flexible. The soul has the freedom to accelerate its levels of growth, and in some cases to muddle through and underachieve. However, the soul is only permitted a clearly defined, limited time between incarnations.

The Law states that as the soul grows within its evolvement, the degree of time that may elapse between incarnations increases. This means that if one has only three or four incarnations left in his pattern, he may elect not to incarnate for many, many hundreds of years. During the earlier and middle levels of growth, the soul must assume incarnations within a specific span of time.

Another Law states: "A soul may not elect to serve a solitary incarnation on a planet unless that incarnation is one of service for his Father."

Within each planet there exists a vibration and pattern of length of incarnations. For example: when a soul begins its first incarnation on the planet Earth, it signs a "contract," so to speak, from forty-eight to seventy-two incarnations, all told. The leeway is there to allow for rapid growth and evolution. This is done to keep harmony within the vibrations of the planet and the societies as well.

A soul may not voluntarily incarnate in a civilization of a lower vibration. The only exception being, if one is acting in the capacity of doing service for the Father, to serve as a conscious master or teacher for the purpose of helping to elevate vibrations on a specific planet. Then, one acts in the capacity of what we know as an "alien soul." In the normal course of evolution, the step-down would upset the balance and equilibrium of the soul and those living on the planet.

Another Law: "If an alien soul involved in a service incarnation in a lower vibration is incapable of completing that incarnation and leaves by any one of a number of methods such as suicide, insanity, or any other abnormal type of departure, the soul is relieved of its responsibility for the service pattern and is allowed to return to the area it came from before the service began."

The reason for this is quite simple. The Father does not wish to punish a soul, nor is it desired to damage the vibrations of a soul. Once this has occurred, it would be necessary for the soul to have extensive retraining before it could successfully re-enter those vibrations, and time does not permit this.

Personality

What role does the soul play in relation to the conscious personality? The Law states: "The soul may in no manner use force or coercion to try to influence the conscious mind in any manner or action. It is the soul's function and responsibility to make the conscious personality aware of its presence, its lessons, and its mission."

This process begins on the first day of birth and continues during the course of the lifetime, mostly at the unconscious level by the implantation of thoughts, reactions, and emotions. It guides the conscious personality toward the desired results, feelings, and successes that the soul wishes to achieve during the lifetime.

The soul tries to make the individual aware, but not by fear or by threats. This would be a karmic situation for the soul as it would be interfering with the free expression of the personality. However, this is done at times, and there are many who are walking the physical plane who seem to be possessed spiritually but who are not possessed. Their own souls are coercing and forcing them into situations in which they do not wish to be involved. For this, the soul shall draw a heavy lesson to itself. The union between the conscious personality and the soul must be accomplished in a Love vibration.

This situation is extremely rare, and only occurs when a soul truly "regrets" an elected incarnation. Circumstances resulting from environmental conditions, physical accidents, and free will may negate the soul's purpose for the expression. This could cause anger by the soul, who may wish to terminate the incarnation earlier than planned.

One may ask, "What if the conscious personality refuses to accept the presence of the soul?" What if it knows that the soul is there and says, "Go away, don't bother me, I wish to have fun and play." Is the soul held responsible for the lack of growth in this case? The answer is yes. For somewhere along the way the soul has neglected to do something it should have done. Somewhere it has not been successful in projecting its love and its understanding to the conscious mind. We know, all of us, that the most powerful tool we have is love. If it does not work, and one does not react positively to it, then it has been improperly applied.

When an individual goes through an incarnation without achieving growth at the conscious level, he finds himself involved in another situation where the soul will assume another incarnation in only a few years. Lack of growth in an incarnation is not a desirable result, and it will be strongly suggested to the soul that it re-enter the physical plane quickly to achieve what it failed to achieve before. It can, in essence, refuse to do this, but that does not occur, as the soul knows that growth must be experienced before its evolution can be advanced.

Hate

The Law states: "When man invokes the emotions and vibrations of total rejection of another human being, or hatred, he shall in his next incarnation be denied the vibrations of love." These vibrations shall not be denied to him for the total incarnation but until the time comes when he realizes the value of the love vibration, and works and earns the right to receive it once again.

It may seem strange to you that your Father would have a Law pertaining to hate, for it is a vibration that is not recognized as being in existence. Yet, it is a vibration that is expressed by man and must be dealt with properly.

The vibrations of hate are those of judgment, almost total judgment. They are also the vibrations of prolonged anger, resentment, and other undesirable qualities. So, the person draws a most severe lesson in return. There are many instances throughout history that are recorded in the vibrations of hate, recorded in heinous acts of violence and crimes against humanity as expressions of this hatred.

The vibrations of hatred are the vibrations of total rejection. It is closing the door on another human being, refusing to attempt to understand his truth. The line is very fine.

How much difference is there between acceptance and rejection? Perhaps the only difference is in your confidence relating to yourselves, which either gives you or denies you the capacity to accept others in their truth.

Acquisition

The Law states: "Anyone may acquire what he has determined is a need for him, to any degree or quantity, as long as it is acquired in good faith, honorably, and through his own efforts."

Out of all of your Father's Laws, perhaps this one has been the most difficult to observe. Man has consistently given himself to the feelings of unworthiness, poverty, and other negative energies. The time has come for all to understand that it is not your Father's desire that you be deprived of anything in order to prove your devotion to Him or to achieve your spiritual growth. It is not necessary for you to incur suffering upon yourself, to feel unworthiness, to feel pain and anguish, or to feel deprivation in order to grow. All you must feel is your Father within.

The ancients tore their clothes and covered themselves with ashes upon the loss of a loved one. This is done to this day in many areas of religious practice. Why should they not rejoice at the return of a child to Spirit? They felt it made them better men to suffer so: they felt it brought them closer to their Father to suffer and bring misery upon themselves and stripped themselves of their possessions. The Holy men were beggars, without assets, wandering from place to place, depending upon the charity of others for their sustenance. This was not proper. This is not the way your Father intends it to be. There is to be joy in your growth. There is to be joy in your acquisition, spiritually as well as physically.

The suffering that man endures is a manifestation of his own creation to prove to himself his unworthiness. Why? Let man prove his worth, not his lack of worth. For only then can he achieve. Under the Law of Acquisition, things acquired in the proper manner and by the proper methods continue to flow, in and out, always being replenished, always being passed on to others. When things are acquired in violation of the Law, the flow stops, suffering endures, and deprivation eventually occurs, for it is a sign of lack of faith.

    Raise your sights in your lives. Do not bend and stoop your shoulders. Do not humble yourself, for there is no one to humble yourself to; only yourself.

Negativity

The Law states: "Negativity is a balancing expression of the Love vibration designed to expose the soul to the spectrum of frequencies involved within an action and a reaction."

It is of the utmost importance that all of my children understand the role that the Laws of Negativity play in your lives, in your growth, and in your evolution. No soul involved within a karmic pattern of growth can achieve communication and oneness with the Father unless it has passed through the Laws of

Negativity and assimilated them. This is Law.

One might say that if your Father is Love, and you are to be Love, why must you suffer? You have been told many times that if you suffer, it is of your own creation. In essence, this is quite true. Being exposed to the Laws of Negativity does not imply that one must suffer, only that one must understand and place the vibration in its proper perspective. The suffering that does occur is to a great degree your own creation, for at the given time you create a need for the suffering. It seems to fit, to be comfortable with the negative expression. Once again, this is a preconditioned habit or attitude that one has assumed through the course of one's life.

The Laws of Negativity create the balance. Without them you could not have your system of action and reaction, of balance and counterbalance, of cause and effect. For if at your level of vibration, and similar levels of vibration throughout this Universe, all was a Love vibration, no growth would occur. If everything were always Truth, growth would be impossible, as there would be no comparison, no way to determine your truth, for everything would be on one side of the scale. There would be no choice, no opportunity for individuality, which would result in lack of freedom of expression.

The basic problem is that most humans relate to negativity as something evil, as something detrimental and to be avoided at all cost. It is time for mankind to understand that negativity is merely a balancing expression. It is a lower vibration of Love, but it is a vibration of Love, for that is all there is.

Let us create an example of an individual who becomes so highly spiritual in his conscious mind that he closes the doors on all vibrations except those of Love. What effect does this have on his life? The major effect is that sooner or later it will place him in a state of isolation where he shall find it impossible to engage in social situations, or even in a controversial conversation where he might find disagreement with his truth. He will have closed off his vibrations to this.

What will happen to this individual? His growth shall stagnate and eventually regress.

This is Universal Law. Growth may not stand still; it moves in one direction or another. How many times have each of you been involved in a situation where something occurred to shock you back to reality when you had been living in a world of dreams or illusions, closing yourself off from the real world? This is not evil, it is constructive.

How do you use negativity in relation to your spiritual growth? It becomes a very important tool in the course of your education and initiations. You have heard the words spoken, that you are often taught in what I refer to as "negative truth," not "lies." How does this work? I shall give you an example.

Suppose one of your masters comes to

you and relates a fact of truth to you unknown to you before. You recognize and accept it as your truth and allow it to become a part of your reality. Once this has been accomplished, the negative vibrations shall begin to flow. They shall try to destroy your belief in the truth you have just acquired. Sincere, strong efforts are made to create doubts in your mind, perhaps to offer you other alternatives to the newly acquired truth. What is the result? There are two results.

The most desirable result is that of your fighting off the negative suggestion, reinforcing your truth, making it stronger and stronger. In the future, when someone challenges this aspect of your truth, you shall stand firm, defend it, and utilize it in your work. This is the purpose for exposing you to the negative expression in that situation—to strengthen your beliefs, to hammer you until you become stronger and stronger.

The other result is that the individual allows the negativity to become dominant and begins to doubt the newly accepted truth and to release it. He then adopts the negative expression as his new truth. What happens then? In many instances that individual is lost to his spirtual path. At times, he will have to begin to learn this situation all over again.

This may seem like a stern measure, but you must understand that before you become consciously One with the vibrations of your Father, He must be firmly convinced of the solidarity of your vibrations and intent. Once you reach the point of no return within your growth, there can be no weakening of your dedication. There can be no saying that you are tired and disgusted and are going to chuck the whole thing. This cannot be allowed to happen. You are in a situation where the strong survive, the strength being your Love for your Father. Strength is accepted growth.

When you have reached a level in your growth where it is time for you to be exposed to negativity, never, never attempt to eliminate it. The key is to recognize the presence of the negative aspect. Once the recognition has taken place, you are to utilize this expression for positive growth, not to be adversely affected by it. Then you do not have to suffer, do not have to experience pain; rather, you become aware that what you call negativity is in reality Love in a different expression. It offers you a choice and helps you ascertain your truth more firmly. It is there to build, not to destroy. No one who walks with his Father is here to destroy.

Once in a while an individual who is not consciously aware will allow himself to be consumed by the negative aspects of vibrations. Sometimes this is initiated at the soul level for purposes of growth within a lesson, but many times it is a decision made by the conscious ego. The individual will then lead his life dominated by a negative vibration. This is not something that has been imposed on him; it is what he has imposed upon himself. The individuals involved in this expression comprise your criminal element, mercenary soldiers, and people who take pleasure in seeing others destroyed and suffering. They have allowed the negative vibration to overshadow the vibrations of Love, throwing their perspectives of life completely out of balance.

Spiritual Law

The words inscribed on the tablets known as the Ten Commandments are Laws relating to man's behavior to his brother and within the structure of the society in which he lives. Truly, some of the Laws, as written at that time, cannot be directly applied at this time. For as societies grow and expand, the Laws also must grow and expand.

The Spiritual Law is indeed contained within the unwritten doctrine known as the Kabala or Cabbalah. It was impossible to have true posterity, for at any given moment mankind was not totally prepared to observe or accept the Law. Each individual must grow into the awareness and acceptance of Spiritual Law individually. Yet, each is eternally subject to the Law. The Law contains the basic foundation and energies under which man commences, and endures, his patterns of lessons and growth. It is the basic guideline under which all souls develop and evolve. I shall begin at the beginning.

REALITY

"Thou shalt not deny the existence of God, for He is your only reality." The Father says to you that I AM, and all else is a variable that changes at all times. Only I AM is a constant. Therefore, when you take it upon yourselves to deny His existence, your total existence becomes a lie. If an individual, during the course of an incarnation, consciously accepts his Father's presence within his being and his life, once accepted it cannot be denied. The rejection of His presence truly draws the most severe lesson to the individual, for it is a total judgment of one's truth, of one's only reality. For this, the individual, within a future incarnation, shall have an intense desire to find the God within and shall have a difficult time in doing so. He shall be denied this opportunity until it is recognized that the desire is totally his truth.

CAUSE AND EFFECT

"For every cause there is an effect." Who has

the ability to create causes? Is this opportunity available to all at any given moment? Most assuredly not. In order to create causes, one must be as one with the I AM within himself. One must walk in his truth, and live it. For the ability to create causes carries with it a weighty responsibility. With each cause created, many, many are affected. You are to say to the Lord your God, "I am You, and You are I, and I have totally accepted your Love and Truth within my vibrations; therefore, I have achieved eternal peace and understanding. All my needs shall be fulfilled, for I am as one with my Father and need have no concerns. This total union has relieved me of all concerns, and when it is proper to create a cause, it shall be done."

ACCEPTANCE

The Law of Acceptance can also be called the Law of Understanding. It is mankind's responsibility to accept the Word of their Father and understand it. This cannot be easily achieved, for during the early stages of growth, mankind finds itself needing to ask why, who, and how. Only upon unification, when one has accepted his oneness, can one also accept the "Word" as just being the "Word."

The stability of growth eliminates the need for labeling and identification. Your Father is the source of your Divine Truth. As you grow and accept your Oneness with Him, all that comes to you is recognized as Truth and just is. . . .

KARMA

I speak to you of opportunities to work out experiences incurred between two souls. The Law is firm. Many times man has said, "I am in misery in my life for a lesson I have incurred with one who is still in spirit form." This is invalid. Vibrations incurred in the physical must be worked out in the physical. Spirit is in a total vibration of Love. A lesson acquired by a soul does not necessarily have to be worked out with the same soul with whom it was incurred. When this is done, it usually is done on a voluntary basis to assist the soul who has incurred the lesson.

JUDGMENT

We talk of the Law, "Thou shalt not judge."

Who plays the role of judge? Do not ask me if your Father sits in judgment, for He has created children of Love who need no judgment. Within the structure of the Law, there is a section relating to total judgment of self. This assumes many forms: insanity, spiritual possession, total failure to accept one's role within society, becoming dependent upon the state for sustenance and survival, and, the most severe form of self-judgment, suicide. What occurs when a soul makes transition and becomes aware of the total judgment it has placed upon itself during the course of an incarnation? It understands what it has done. It elects to work out these vibrations as rapidly as possible, for this type of lesson cannot be carried forth for great periods of time.

For example, the soul may incarnate with suicidal tendencies until the person is thirty-five years of age. If the individual displays the strength to overcome the tendencies and survives, the karma is fulfilled and peace enters the balance of the life.

SOUL EVOLUTION

We talk of the Law pertaining to soul evolution. The Law states that when a soul has evolved to a predetermined level it has earned the right to end its series of karmic physical incarnations and assimilate within the vibrations of the Spirit Core. At that point, it is the soul's choice either to immediately begin new levels of evolution, or to voluntarily remain within the present vibrations to do service in assisting other souls who have not yet completed their patterns. A soul may not avoid its obligations of growth. A soul may not defer serious infractions that have incurred lessons for itself. A soul may not interfere with the normal course of vibrations within a civilization on any occupied planet. A soul, whether in spirit or physical form, may not cross over and interfere in other spheres of vibrations without requesting permission to do so.

SPIRITUAL FIDELITY

We talk of the Law of Spiritual Fidelity. Whom does it pertain to? Does it pertain to souls that have established a union of vibrations for themselves? Or does it pertain only to the soul and its Father? For as it was written on the tablets given to Moses, "Thou shalt have no other gods before me."

The words I have spoken to you to this point have been passed down from initiate to initiate for many thousands of years. Within their rigidity, they have expanded, become flexible to accommodate the needs of more highly evolved civilizations and societies. The basic foundation remains unchanged; it is only the scope that broadens and expands. It was totally to this purpose that the Ten Commandments were released to the ancient Hebrews. The Law is the Law, and those who do not follow its path account to themselves for their digressions. You must understand that what befalls mankind he places upon himself, that what occurs to man that is not godly he has requested.

A soul is created in Love, nurtured and developed to grow in Love, to become aware in Oneness with the I AM. Strive for this in your growth, release those in your lives who prohibit and deter you from finding this Oneness, for this is your destiny, and
I bless you.

CHRIST LIGHT

When one recognizes and accepts the presence of the Universal Christ Light within him, then he shall have made available to him the use of the Light and the Love to assist him in his work. If the belief and the acceptance are not there, it shall not flow for him, for there is no halfway measure. One either accepts the Light or denies its existence. One cannot call upon God on Mondays, Wednesdays, and Fridays.

Ten Commandments

Understand that at the time the Ten Commandments were handed down, the responsibility that man was aware of bears little relation to the responsibility of the Children of Light at this time. Therefore, the interpretation of the Commandments, of necessity, was quite different from what it will be at this date. Let us begin.

1

"I am the Lord your God who brought you out of Egypt, out of the land of slavery. You shall have no other Gods before me."

If this Law were to be written at the present time, the wording would have to be drastically changed, for by and large mankind no longer worships idols, mythological gods, or planets and the stars. Man worships his Father and is aware of the role that his Father plays in his life. Even those who claim to be atheists do so because they do not wish to believe in the Father, but do not create an idol imagery or another form of spirit to worship, and so, in essence, they are acknowledging the existence of their Father, even though they are denying it.

Today, perhaps this Commandment might say, "I am the Lord your God. Thou shalt place no other want, desire, or need before

Me, for I AM, and I AM all that is." If we were to word this in this manner, what we basically would be saying is that man should use caution not to place his greed, his emotional desires, his ego desires in front of his recognition of his Father and the God within. One could say that man, on occasion, uses these expressions as idols and lower gods and worships them. To a degree this is true, but it is not complete, for even at that point he recognizes the existence of his Father. When it is said to you, "I am the Lord your God," it is also saying to you, "recognize Me, for I am within you, and We are as One, and therefore you cannot deny My existence, for in doing so you deny yours, and you cannot place anything or anyone above Me, for in doing so you place them above yourself."

2

"You shall not make for yourself an idol in the form of Heaven above, or on the Earth beneath, or in the waters below. You shall not bow down to them or worship them, for I, the Lord your God, am a jealous God, punishing the children for the sins of the fathers to the third and fourth generation of those who hate me, but showing love to thousands who love Me and keep My Commandments."

In reading this Commandment, there is one word that stands out like a sore thumb, and the word is **jealous**, where it says, "and I am a jealous God." If man accepts the fact that He is a jealous God, then the next thought in your mind must be, "A jealous God is quick to anger and quick to seek revenge. A jealous God will act irrationally, and harm will result."

Was the purpose of the wording of this Commandment to actually relate to man that God is jealous? Or was the function of this Commandment to say, "Tow the mark, stay in line, do not incur the wrath of your Father." Or was it, perhaps, man's own fear? Could it have been that man felt that if he erred and strayed, indeed the wrath of God would come down upon his head? If we were to rewrite this Commandment this day, perhaps it would sound like this: "I am the Lord your God. I am Love and Light. I am All Seeing,

All Knowing, and All Benevolent, and I allow you the freedom of choice and freedom of will to take any action you wish during the course of your lives, as long as you also take responsibility for the results of your actions. If you wish to err, I bless you and charge you with the responsibility to learn from the error, but the choice is yours."

    Here we have a very different set of circumstances. In the original wording, the responsibility for the action is not man's, but our Father's. The thought was that if man does not do as his Father wishes him to do, he shall incur His wrath. If man does it, and it turns out wrong, then the Father has guided and steered man incorrectly and it is not our responsibility.

If we look at the rewording of this Law, we find that we are assuming responsibility for our actions, our thoughts, our ideas, for we have reached the point in our evolution where we are capable of handling this type of responsibility and accounting to ourselves for our actions. We know that we are responsible to ourselves and that our Father, in His benevolence, allows us to take our actions no matter what they be, if they are our truth.

3

"You shall not misuse the Name of the Lord your God, for the Lord will not hold anyone guiltless who misuses His Name."

Perhaps we could say this another way: "Thou shalt not use the Name of the Lord thy

God in vain." What was the purpose of this Law? Was it handed down to create respect for the Father? Was it handed down so that man should be in fear that he dare not write or pronounce the Name of God? Was it handed down so that man should not cover his feet or bare his head in the presence of the energies of his Father, to show that he is inferior to Him?

These were many of the results of the interpretation of this Law. If I were to say to you, "Thou shalt not take thy name in vain; thou shalt not hold thyself in ridicule; thou shalt not hold thyself in shame," I am saying the same thing. The only variation is that I am holding you accountable to yourselves. I am demanding that you recognize the God within. I am saying to you that when you hold your Father in awe, you are holding yourself in awe of self. When you deny yourself spiritual love, you are denying this love to your Father, and when you are denying it to your Father you are denying it to yourself.

Once again we have thrown the responsibility for this Commandment back into your hands. You become responsible for it in relation to yourself.

4

"Observe the Sabbath Day by keeping it Holy as the Lord your God has commanded you. Six days shall you labor and do all your work, but the evening and seventh day is a Sabbath to the Lord your God. On it you shall not do any work, neither you, nor your son or daughter, nor your manservant nor your maidservant nor your ox nor your donkey, or any of your animals, nor the aliens within your gates, so that your manservants and maidservants may rest as you do. Remember that you were slaves in Egypt and that the Lord your God brought you out of there with a mighty hand and an outstretched arm. Therefore, the Lord your God has commanded you to observe the Sabbath Day."

I would be saying the same thing to you if I said: "You may work for six days, but you will rest your body and your mind on the seventh day, for if you do not, you shall draw a lesson to yourself." Why would this be so?

There is a Universal Law that applies to the proper care and the proper concern for the physical vehicle while you are in a physical incarnation. You cannot disregard its existence. If you strain and push yourself to the point of exhaustion so that your physical structure becomes weak and diseased, you shall draw a lesson to yourself.

Let me rephrase the Law for you: "Labor for six days, and on the seventh, contemplate your growth, care for yourself, nurture and love yourself. Bless your Father for giving you the strength to put forth effort for growth during the past six days. Recharge your bodies and your minds so that you may undertake a new week with vigor and strength."

Man truly did not understand the reason

for resting on the Sabbath. He did not understand that the seventh day, the day of rest, was time to be put aside to love himself, to be aware of himself, to care for himself. It was put to him in such a manner that he thought that the seventh day was to be one of servitude to the Father, almost a type of punishment, that he had to forgo pleasures and true needs, when this was not the case. The Holy Temple is within, and it must be cared for.

5

"Honor your Father and your Mother as the Lord your God has commanded you, so that you may live long, so that it may go well with you in the land the Lord your God is giving you."

The key word in this Law is **honor**. What does the word **honor** mean? I venture to say there is quite a difference in the meaning today from what it was many thousands of years ago. The wording of the Law need not be changed, it is just the understanding of the meaning of the word **honor**. Honor does not mean servitude. Honor does not mean blind obedience or denial of one's own needs. It does not mean the subjugation of one's personality to another.

These are the interpretations that were assigned to this word in ancient times, for man and woman sacrificed of themselves to the greatest degree to honor their mother and their father. The phrase, "honor thy mother and thy father," could be restated as, "honor thy brothers and thy sisters." Then perhaps we could have the true meaning of this Law. It could also mean, "honor the heavens and the Earth, care for what your Father has given you, respect it, recognize its existence."

Thy Mother, thy Father, and Thyself. The Trinity; the male, the female, and the love. The word **honor** in the present context means recognition, respect, and acceptance, and we need not go further than those three words. It is also not our role to be possessed by anyone, only to acknowledge their existence, to respect their position and their beliefs, and to recognize them as a brother or sister. If we can achieve this, then we truly can have a free relationship with all mankind, without drawing to ourselves guilt for actions not taken, whether they be our truth or not. We do not take to ourselves obligations that are not ours of our own choice. We do not feel weighted down with the responsibilities of others when it is not our desire to accept these responsibilities. Honor thy mother and thy father, but do it in the broadest sense of the term.

6

"You shall not commit murder."

This Commandment was uttered in five words. It would be difficult to change these five words to modernize this Law, and yet perhaps it could be done.

Perhaps we could say, "Thou shalt not

make total judgment on a brother or sister."

Why was it necessary to have this Commandment? If man walked with his Father, then surely he walked in Love and surely he valued life, but it seems that the value that man placed on life was quite different from the value that you place on life today. Why was this so? Was it because man was permitted to have more than one and knew in his mind that life was eternal? Was it because what we call the Laws of Exchange were unknown at that time?

If we look at this Law in the context of our awareness today, perhaps we can see that "thou shalt not murder" may apply to more than just the slaying of another human being. "Thou shalt not murder another's ambition; thou shalt not murder another's desire; thou shalt not murder thy love for thy Father."

To murder is to slay, to end a cycle. The Law was not worded, "Thou shalt not cause death," for there is no death. Who are we to determine that the time for the ending of another's cycle has come? We must also be aware that this Law encompasses what is known as suicide, for that is also murder. If we are a projection of our Father, then the life is not ours to take, even if it is our own.

7

"Thou shalt not commit adultery."

If two people are in business and are competitors, and one approaches a valued employee of the other and offers him an inducement to lure him away from his employer, this is adultery. If a person bribes an employee of another concern to reveal secrets relating to the scope and area of the business, this is adultery.

At the time the Commandments were originally handed down, man was in many respects a carnal being. Many times throughout history there have been recorded civilizations and cities that were totally carnal in nature. Perhaps this Commandment should have been stated, "Thou shalt have respect for others," but when we are referring to people we cannot say, "Thou shalt respect others' possessions," for no man possesses another.

In ancient times the moral codes were almost nonexistent, so stringent Laws had to be established to enable some form of structure of society to exist, to have some sort of law and order.

What is adultery? The word **adult** means ripe, mature. Are we saying that two mature adults may not have a relationship and share each other if it is their desire to do so? Perhaps the word **adultery** should be changed to the word **rape**, for then we would have the desire and consent of one adult and not the other, and then we would be committing murder. The true definement of the Law of Adultery has been hampered greatly by churches of all faiths and all religions for fear that society would once again turn carnal.

Responsibilities would be thrown to the wind and mankind would once again become savage. If this is man's choice, then let it be so.

If a man and a man, a woman and a woman, or a man and a woman are involved with each other in any type of relationship of an intimate nature of their own free will and desire, then they, and they alone, must assume the responsibility for their actions. If they take this action, and it is in their truth at all levels of awareness, then they have committed nothing but a union. However, we now reach the fine line, for if in living and enacting their truth it causes harm or damage to another human being, and this damage is the result of a breach of contract, then the responsibility for this damage falls upon them.

It is easy to say, "Well, the injured party must learn his own lesson," but if it is a lesson that he has not asked for, then it is not his, it has been cast upon him without his desire. Many times some of you have said, "Will the time come in the world when marriage, as it is known today, will cease to exist?" This is very possible, for no child of God possesses another, no enlightened child wishes to have limits and restrictions placed upon his expressions.

I am not saying that the institution of family life will disappear. I am saying that there shall be more peace and harmony. I am saying that there shall be less turmoil, for all mankind will acknowledge that they are free. When they enter into a relationship, they shall do so because it is their own desire to do so, not out of pressure from family, from society, or to place a label on themselves.

Would that not be adultery? Adultery is a rape, a lack of truth, a destruction of truth. But it can only be incurred if one of the parties involved acknowledges that the act he is about to undertake is one to be feared, to be ashamed of, and to undertake in guilt. We do not feel guilty for actions we take in our truth; we feel joy and love. So, we say to you that an adulterer is, in essence, a murderer, a rapist, for he strips away his truth to perform an action.

8

"Thou shalt not steal."

If a child is starving, and takes for himself a slice of bread, is that stealing? What is stealing? The dictionary says that stealing is the acquiring of something that is not yours by illegal methods. If this is so, then we have two categories of stealing. We have stealing relating to physical things, and stealing relating to spiritual things.

How can one steal if one owns nothing, for there would be nothing to steal.

How could you take something from me, have me say that you have stolen it, when nothing is mine, for I own nothing. Perhaps we could try to reword this Commandment to say, " Thou shalt not acquire things by reason of greed." What does one do when one steals something? He stops the flow, for he desires more than is flowing to him, and it does not matter what the purpose is. It does not matter if it is to retain it, to resell it, or to use it to acquire other means of exchange.

"Thou shalt not steal." You are all children of God. You are as our Father. You are flowing Light that is in constant movement to you, passing through, and coming to you again. Yet, I have seen those children on their path of growth who, when they see another individual reaching a point in his evolution that has been denied themselves, look for ways to reach that point, look to see what that individual has done. They look to see what he has acquired so that they may "steal" it, so that they too shall be as he is.

What do we do with people who are what we call "energy parasites," who try to read and drain people's minds, who try to use their power to control people's lives and get them to do their bidding, who form cults to brainwash others? These people are spiritual thieves, for they are taking what belongs to God.

Many Children of Light are channels for specific areas of information and enlightenment. Their role is to share this information with their brothers and sisters, much as we are doing in this book. Yet, there are some who feel that what has come to them is theirs, and they will use it to make their fame and fortune. They attempt to steal the knowledge, the techniques, and the methods from the Father and declare them to be their own, when in truth they own nothing, and their flow stops.

It is impossible to steal, for there is nothing to steal, as he who holds on and says, "I have been robbed," is unaware that he had nothing in the first place.

9

"Thou shalt not bear false witness against thy neighbor."

When the ancients bore false witness against their neighbors, they suffered the pangs of guilt and remorse. In the broadening of the interpretation of these words, let us include: "Thou shalt not lead the minds of others astray by relating personal judgments against thy neighbors." Merely gossiping gives false testimony against thy neighbor. Certainly, relating your decision to another moves from decision to judgment, and that is false witness.

Man is always entitled to his opinions and decisions pertaining to his personal involvement with another. This becomes false testimony and judgment when it is related to another who is not involved in the action.

10

"Thou shalt not covet your neighbor's wife. Thou shalt not set your desires on your neighbor's house, or land, his servants, his animals, or anything that belongs to your neighbor."

What does the word **covet** mean? Does it mean that man is to be without feelings and emotions, without desires? Most of mankind, when he reads this Law, remembers only, "Thou shalt not covet thy neighbor's wife," and forgets the balance of the Commandment. Man tends to feel that the balance applied only during ancient times, so let's reword it. "Do not covet thy neighbor's twelve-room house, his Rolls-Royce, his swimming pool, his butler, etc." This man can relate to!

On the other hand, if you do not desire, you do not grow. What is the difference between the words **admire** and **desire**? If you admire another man's wife, does that mean you are coveting her? If you desire her, and allow her to become aware of your feelings, then you are coveting her, for you have taken an action upon a thought.

If one could not dream, if one could not imagine, if one could not place himself in magical situations to allow his mind to roam, to wonder, to experiment and to create, then indeed he would be in a sorry state of affairs. To fantasize is not to covet; many times it is a stimulus for one to create his own and do for himself. To covet is to desire, but to desire to such an extent that it interferes with the normal course of life and becomes an all-consuming passion is the error.

You learn that we are not to become attached to material things, that they are transitory and you must be capable of releasing them at a moment's notice. Take an Earth-bound soul that has passed and that is bound here because it cannot bear to leave its possessions. It cannot bear to leave its beautiful home, its lovely furnishings and other things that it loves so much. Is the soul not desiring these things out of proportion and reason?

So, perhaps we should rewrite this Law and say, "Do not covet what is not yours, and have the faith and knowledge that the flow of life shall provide you with your needs and, if you are lucky enough, with some of your desires as well."

Do not allow the connotation of the word **covet** to be a restriction upon your freedom of expression and upon your growth.

Do not be afraid to approach someone with whom you could have an interchange of energy, of knowledge, of growth, for fear that others may talk or frown upon this association.

Covet thy Father, and His Light, and His Love and His Knowledge. Allow the rest of the world to flow to you and through you.

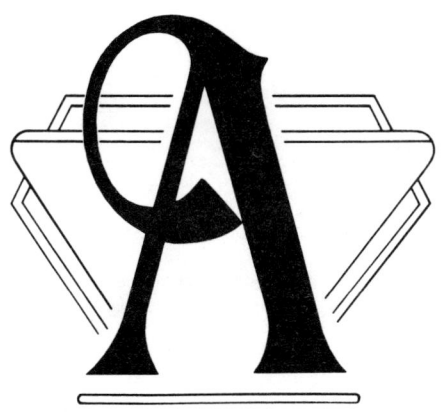

Dr. Frank Alper

BOOKS
TAPES
LECTURE
SERIES

From
The Arizona Metaphysical Society

EXPLORING ATLANTIS

BOOKS
Volumes I, II, III   **$11.95 each**

A "Journey Through Time" with Dr. Frank Alper. This material deals with ancient Atlantis and Crystal Healing. The Great Healing Temple. The Temple of the Dolphins. The Hall of Justice. Magnetic Energies. Crystals and Patterns for healing, as well as other experimental civilizations.

VIDEO   **$49.95**
VHS or BETA available, please specify

A two-hour video "Journey Through Time" with Dr. Frank Alper. In this unique video cassette, Dr. Alper ties together for the first time, the moral, social, cultural and economic practices and philosophies of Ancient Atlantis. He correlates the priorities that mankind faces today, how we can rise above destruction and utilize this knowledge to bring mankind into this age of enlightenment.

HEALING WITH CRYSTALS

VIDEO **$49.95**
VHS or BETA available, please specify

A Video Program with Dr. Frank Alper showing his healing techniques with crystals.

Dr. Frank Alper has long been considered the pioneer in healing with magnetic energies using geometric configurations. This video tape shows the placement and the way to use crystals for healing as well as the means for giving new energies to the places where they are needed most.

AUDIO CASSETTES
CRYSTALS, COLOR AND SOUND (seven tape set,
6½ hours) **$55.00**
A taped seminar dealing with crystals, color and sound.

AUDIO CASSETTES

The Atlantean Chants — $7.95
Twenty-four chants of ancient Atlantean vibrations that pertain to growth and evolvement.

Murvin—Commander of Jupiter I — $9.95
An interview with Murvin, who describes the space brothers, life and purpose aboard ship.

The Twelve Disciples — $9.95
Channeled by the energies of Peter and the Father.

Solomon: Universal Consciousness — $9.95
How to achieve Universal Consciousness. Includes a guided meditation by Solomon.

Conditioning the Child of Light — $9.95
How to survive and relate to society from your spiritual essence.

Success and Failure Mechanisms — $9.95
Determine your mind orientation relating to goal achievement and balance.

Removing Emotional and Sexual Blocks — $9.95
Tools to help you relive self-imposed blocks that hamper fulfillment.

The Golden Triad — $9.95
The energies of the Age of Aquarius. The power of the energies of creative matter.

The Word — $7.95
A description of the symbolic twenty-two steps of Karmic evolution.

Universal Law (two tape set) — $14.95
Over thirty Universal Laws are channeled and described by the energies of the Father.

The Twelve Initiations (two tape set) — $14.95
A description of the physical and spiritual initiations of the soul.

BOOKS

Moses and the Bible (volumes I–IV) — $11.95
A spiritual interpretation of Creation and the written word. The Old and New Testaments. Ancient civilizations on and inside the earth, spiritual laws, the Ten Commandments, and much more.

"An Evening With Christos" (volumes I–V) — $11.95
A year of monthly spiritual channelings consisting of a lecture, followed by questions and answers. The energies of many masters have contributed to these timeless volumes.

Universal Healing Rays (pamphlet) — $1.00

THE CONTINUING TAPE SERIES

Quarterly — $24.00
Semi-Annually — $45.00
Annually — $84.00

The spiritual teachings of Dr. Frank Alper are now available on sixty-minute tapes. Each month you will receive new information for your growth and evolution.

The tapes will contain information pertaining to the new energies of the Aquarian age, coming spiritual awakenings and events, higher interpretations of many basic laws of spiritual life and much more.

This program will enable you to continue your growth in a progressive manner, with new stimuli.

The program may be subscribed to on a quarterly, semi-annual, or annual basis.

PAST SUBJECTS INCLUDE:

Karma, Love & Detachment	Planetary Evolution
Truth & Responsibility	Universal Creation
The Union of Marriage	Male & Female Energies
Spiritual Path vs. Religion	The Initiation of Fire
Learning to Channel	Building Confidence
Coping with Spiritual & Sexual Stress	

Any of the above tapes may be ordered singly — **$9.95 each**

Order Form	Cost	Qty.	T
BOOKS			
EXPLORING ATLANTIS I II III (Circle Choices)	$11.95 ea.		
EVENING WITH CHRISTOS I II III IV V (Circle Choices)	$11.95 ea.		
MOSES AND THE BIBLE I II III IV (Circle Choices)	$11.95 ea.		
UNIVERSAL HEALING RAYS	$ 2.00		
VIDEO TAPES			
EXPLORING ATLANTIS, VHS or BETA (Circle One)	$49.95		
HEALING WITH CRYSTALS, VHS or BETA (Circle One)	$49.95		
AUDIO CASSETTES			
ATLANTEAN CHANTS	$ 7.95		
MURVIN	$ 9.95		
TWELVE DISCIPLES	$ 9.95		
SOLOMON	$ 9.95		
THE CHILD OF LIGHT	$ 9.95		
UNIVERSAL LAW (2 tape set)	$14.95		
THE GOLDEN TRIAD	$ 9.95		
CRYSTALS, COLOR AND SOUND (7 tape set)	$55.00		
TWELVE INITIATIONS (2 tape set)	$14.95		
THE WORD	$ 7.95		
SUCCESS AND FAILURE MECHANISMS	$ 9.95		
REMOVING EMOTIONAL & SEXUAL BLOCKS	$ 9.95		
TAPE SERIES			
Quarterly Basis $24.00 Semi-Annually $45.00 Annually $84.00			
INDIVIDUAL TAPES (List your choices on a separate paper)	$ 9.95 ea.		
SUB TOTAL			
POSTAGE			
TOTAL			

- **Handling charges applicable to all orders**
  - $ 0.01–$10.00 . . . . add $1.00
  - $10.01–20.00 . . . . add $2.00
  - $20.01–$30.00 . . . . add $3.00
  - $30.01–$50.00 . . . . add $4.00
  - $50.01–$100.00 . . . . add $5.00
  - $100 and up . . . . add $7.00

  Handling charges and prices subject to change without notice.

- **Canada and Mexico**
  Add $1.00 to each printed handling charge

- **Orders outside of North America.**
  For Surface Mail, add ten percent (10%) of your total order to the printed handling charge.
  For AIR MIAL, add thirty percent (30%) of your total order to the printed handling charge

- Please allow 2–4 weeks for delivery
- U.S. funds only
- No credit cards

Make checks payable to:
Arizona Metaphysical Society
P.O. Box 44027
Phoenix, AZ 85064

Name

Address

City

State   Zip

Phone (   )